Practical
PATIENCE

By

Marc Royer Ph.D.

Practical
Patience

Copyright 1999
Marc Royer
First Printing 1999

Published by:
The Christian Resource Group
11664 Red Oak Dr.
Granger, IN 46530
(219) 273-6235

ISBN: 0-7392-0083-6

Library of Congress Catalog Card Number: 99-93009

Printed in the USA by

MORRIS PUBLISHING
3212 East Highway 30 • Kearney, NE 68847 • 1-800-650-7888

PATIENCE

TABLE OF CONTENTS

Chapter 1: Let Endurance Build Patience

Galatians 6:9--Let us not become weary in doing good, for at the proper time we will reap a harvest if we do not give up.

Patience is not natural to any person. It is something that needs time to develop and grow. A person can learn a lot more from failure than success because someone who has experienced failure is more willing to listen and to learn.

Because we are usually only willing to listen after failure, we don't identify the need to develop patience until it is right upon us. One of the greatest places to start developing patience is **endurance**. Endurance builds patience because it requires sticking with something to see it through. When you stick with something and see it through, you will be less likely to consider quitting the next time the tough times come. If you stick with anything you are doing, you will begin to experience growth in your inner life. One of those areas of growth will be patience.

Paul, in this short message in Galatians, encourages believers to not become weary. Sometimes body chemistry can alter emotional patterns. Sometimes body chemistry and emotions are so interwoven that it becomes difficult to define the problem that is causing weariness.

Not long ago I was with a man who made an interesting announcement to me. He told me to please forgive him if he seemed grouchy for the next few minutes. At the same time he popped a chocolate in his mouth. Through natural curiosity I found out that he was diabetic. When his blood sugar dropped, he felt faint and it would affect his temperament. Chocolate, cheese, or juice would cure the problem temporarily until he could eat lunch. Every morning and evening he would take an insulin injection to help keep his problem under control. Body chemistry altered his emotional pattern.

A friend of mine had terminal cancer. He had no appetite and would get sick if he ate anything. The only thing he could tolerate was just a little Carnation Instant Breakfast Drink from time to time. Due to lack of nourishment, he lost weight and became weaker and weaker. He eventually would become so weak, that his wife would take him to the hospital. They would hook up an "IV" and a special mixture to give him nourishment. Almost immediately my friend would perk up. After a few days he would become strong enough to go home. Once home, he would again become weak and have to return to the hospital for the same treatment.

Emotional difficulties can often drain us the same way a physical problem can. Situations involving a lot of emotional energy can keep us exhausted and worn out for periods of time.

There is a newer disease recently identified that causes complete physical and mental exhaustion. It has been called "baby boomers" disease. Doctors don't know what causes it yet. They think it starts mentally and manifests itself physically. So far, treatment of this disease is limited. People suffering from this disease feel a desperate need to sleep, but when they lie down, sleep doesn't come. This continues until the body is worn out and the mind is weary. The "baby boomers" disease is degenerative. Other sicknesses and diseases often emerge out of this initial ailment.

HAVE YOU EVER BEEN SO EXHAUSTED THAT YOU DID AND SAID THINGS OUT OF CHARACTER FOR YOU?

If you have ever been in need of some rest but had to go out because of a commitment, you have experienced burnout. Burnout can occur in any area of life. Job burnout is one reason for unemployment because attitude affects productivity. Marital burnout is the reason for many divorces. Husbands and wives grow apart and begin to pick at each other. They fuss and argue. They begin to resent each other and finally tear each other apart and call it quits. This scenario is repeated time and again in marriages, workplaces, friendships, and churches. Yet, it does not have to happen this way. If we could only get our exhaustion under control life could be happier and more peaceful.

The nitroglycerine pill brings people great relief when they are experiencing heart pain. People who are weary and exhausted with life need the same kind of relief.

There is no pill to be taken when you are tired of being fair, being good, or being the one always going the extra mile. People sometimes feel so tired and burned out they would like to step aside and let someone else work or help out. Children caring for an ailing adult parent often echo this feeling. Their exhaustion is often only eclipsed by the guilt of their own inner feelings of resentment toward their sick parent. This feeling is echoed again by the nurse who is worn out by the end of the day nursing patients in pain, completing mounds of paper work, and dealing with short-tempered doctors. This sentiment is also echoed by the Sunday school teacher who faithfully prepares a lesson Sunday after Sunday when only a few bother to show up. The list goes on and on--many times a day, in many different ways. We end up exhausted, tired, bored, weak and burned out.

"Weariness" is in essence "weakness." Often we are too prideful to admit weariness is over taking us. Even the effort it takes to put up a front can zap your energy. The energy required to put up a front will wear you down even more.

It is better to face the problem of weariness early. Admit you are in a weakened condition and analyze why you are in this situation. Patience can be developed as you evaluate yourself and your situation. Patience is not natural to anyone who lives in this world. When you become worn out, you will not have the energy left to develop patience. Instead, weariness leaves you feeling trapped, lonely, and abandoned by people who actually love you. When this condition of weariness develops, you are not open to the help of others. Stop and allow these principles work for you.

> **THERE ARE FIVE IMPORTANT PRINCIPLES TO APPLY TO YOUR LIFE TO LET ENDURANCE DEVELOP PATIENCE IN YOU!**

PRINCIPLE #1: ANALYZE AND EVALUATE YOUR COMMITMENTS

Remind yourself that you committed yourself to this project, situation or relationship. There was a reason you committed. Go back and try to remember why. Does this reason still hold ground? If it does, stick with it all the way. Let endurance build patience in your inner life. Remind yourself that the reason you committed yourself to this thing at hand is the same today.

If things have changed in your life and you are hanging on to the commitment before you for unknown reasons, now is the time for evaluation. You must delve into the reason why you are holding on to the commitment. It might be that you would be best to lay this thing aside. This suggestion is not something to take lightly. If you were going back on a commitment in your life just because you are a little uncomfortable, you would be going back on a commitment for the wrong reason.

One thing about commitments is--things do change--we have to change with them. If you are holding on to a commitment just because you don't want to hurt someone's feelings by backing out, you are setting yourself up for burnout.

You may have made a commitment to someone or something and you know you need to follow through, but have lost the vision, energy or excitement. Now is the time to go back to the excitement of the beginning and find out what it was that got you hyped up in the first place. You may need to take a short break and hit it again. Most weariness and exhaustion can be solved by taking a couple of days off. At least you should take a break from something before quitting altogether so you can see if the situation you are facing is really the thing draining you.

PRINCIPLE #2: DEVELOP AN ACCOUNTABILITY TO OTHERS

Weaknesses develop when you don't have others around you to help build you up. Exhaustion occurs when you feel alone and frustrated. We all need each other. No one can handle everything by himself or herself. Most strength comes through encouragement by others.

People under stress often alienate those around them. They say and do things that cause others to stay away. People stay away because they don't want to be turned down. They stay away to protect themselves from emotional harm.

We need people around us who build us up (and we build them up). This kind of encouragement leads to a nurturing environment for people. These are the people we should be honest with in regard to our feelings. We shouldn't keep our weariness and exhaustion from them, but allow it to be exposed. Let people encourage you, counsel you, and advise you. This is what being accountable is all about. Being accountable does not mean you are opening yourself up to being pounded or torn down by a bunch of people. Accountability should exist to help keep each other headed in the right direction, not to scrutinize and criticize each other.

Marriage is the most important accountability unit. Communication is imperative to accountability. It helps people develop the depth of realness needed to endure life.

People with addictions need therapy and group meetings to publicly testify to their abstaining from the addiction.

PRINCIPLE #3: YOU WILL REAP WHAT YOU SOW

Borrowed from agriculture, this principle is an important concept in considering both the quantity and the quality of our effort. There is an unwritten law of the world that says if we sow good seeds consistently we will reap a bountiful harvest. If we sow good seeds, the crop will be good. If we sow bad seeds, the crop will be bad.

This idea has some practical applications. If you develop bad habits you will reap bad health. If you spend all your time building your career but ignore your family, you may be highly successful in your career but have no relationship with your wife and children. Parents who work, work, work, often lament years later when they produce children who are not mature or balanced in their personal lives.

Patience is the key to planting good seed. There are no short cuts in life. There is no substitute for good planting. Consistent, steady and patient effort is what brings the greatest success. Don't look for the quick harvest. It never lasts. The fast money comes and goes. The lessons you learn from life will help you grow and build and become stronger.

There was a farmer in the Midwest who heard he could make $100,000 from a few acres of artichokes. There was supposed to be three markets for them. The vegetable company wanted the root of the plant. A rope company wanted the stalk. A fertilizer company would buy the top. The farmer planted 80 acres because the local elevator promised to buy a special kind of harvester if he bought the seeds from them. The artichokes grew well. They were over eight feet tall. When the time came for harvest, the elevator wouldn't buy the harvester. Further, the vegetable company wasn't interested, and the

Rope Company had gone out of business. Those eighty acres of artichokes rotted in the field. The harvest didn't come because it was all based on making a fortune more than supplying a need. **No matter what you do, you will always reap what you sow.**

Some people work jobs that go nowhere their whole lives. They barely make ends meet, but they keep going. Others lose their relationship with children for years. They keep hoping for a break through, but it never comes. People like this blame themselves in their personal moments taking the responsibility for how things turned out. The thing to remember is--it is not done yet! Keep sowing a positive attitude and reaching out to others and you will yield great harvest. It may not come when you want it to, but it will come.

PRINCIPLE #4: DON'T GIVE UP HOPE

Becoming weary, weak, and exhausted can be a degenerative problem. As we become weaker, it affects our attitude. When our attitude becomes completely negative, it makes a whole situation all that much worse. People don't want to be around you when you are negative. Negativity creates more weakness.

No matter what the task is, don't give up hope. Giving up hope in the middle of something is far worse than never starting it.

Giving up hope is the pinnacle of exhaustion. We simply must not allow ourselves to become so tired and worn out facing an issue that we lose hope. Allow yourself time off or time away from your concerns. Do this on a regular basis. If the concern comes back into your mind while you are taking a break from it, tell it to leave. You have a right to permit yourself time off and time away.

People who are losing their hope are very impatient. They often feel like something is leaving them, but can't put their finger on what it is. This feeling of losing hope is like losing your grip. There are some levels of panic involved at the point of losing your hope.

The best thing to do when you feel like you are loosing your grip is take a step back--take a breath--renew your hope that everything will turn out all right. Concentrate on letting endurance build your patience. Don't give up hope.

PRINCIPLE #5: DO WHATEVER IS NECESSARY TO GIVE YOURSELF A BOOST

Everyone needs time off. Time off has a way of putting things back into perspective. Taking a break helps your endurance and builds your patience.

We all need a boost to our psyches once in a while. Whether it is a good meal or a note of encouragement, we need those things that will perk us up.

Not getting perked up once in a while is like running your gas tank on empty. If you don't refuel, you are going to break down.

Drug addicts shoot all kinds of things into their veins that are slowly poisoning them. The transformation seen in drug addicts who just "shot up" is amazing. The thing killing them is the thing making them feel great for a moment. Drug addicts will do about anything just to get the drugs to get high.

The greatest boost anyone can experience is by turning over his or her situations to a higher power. A non-Christian man was sitting in the lobby of a jail trying to get a top-producing salesman under his department out of jail. He was waiting to go into a preliminary hearing where his employee was charged with kidnapping his girlfriend. The young man displayed a violent temper but made his company a fortune because of his ability to sell. Out of the blue the non-Christian employer said to the Pastor sitting next to him--"What George needs is to give his problems over to Jesus!"

When things close in on you and you feel trapped, you need to develop the habit of turning the problem over to and releasing them to God. The most helpful way of doing this is to close your eyes and visualize yourself actually handing the problem over to God.

Emotionally volatile people are the ones most in need of a boost. Doctors tell us these people are at risk for heart disease, hypertension, and many other potentially fatal sicknesses. Learning to control one's emotions and reactions can actually save one's life. The sooner these people can learn to turn the control of things over to God, the sooner they will lead healthier lives.

LET ENDURANCE BUILD PATIENCE BY APPLYING THESE FIVE PRINCIPLES:

❑ **ANALYZE AND EVALUATE YOUR COMMITMENTS.**

❑ **DEVELOP ACCOUNTABILITY TO OTHERS.**

❑ **REALIZE YOU REAP WHAT YOU SOW.**

❑ **DON'T GIVE UP ON HOPE.**

❑ **DO WHATEVER YOU NEED TO DO TO TURN YOUR SITUATION OVER TO GOD --AND GET A "BOOST".**

CHAPTER 2: LEARNING HOW TO BALANCE ACHIEVEMENT

Psalm 37:1-11 Do not fret because of evil men or be envious of those who do wrong for like the grass they will soon wither, like green plants they will soon die away. Trust in the LORD and do good; dwell in the land and enjoy safe pasture. Delight yourself in the LORD and he will give you the desires of your heart. Commit your way to the LORD; trust in him and he will do this: He will make your righteousness shine like the dawn, the justice of your cause like the noonday sun. Be still before the LORD and wait patiently for him; do not fret when men succeed in their ways, when they carry out their wicked schemes. Refrain from anger and turn from wrath; do not fret-- it leads only to evil. For evil men will be cut off, but those who hope in the LORD will inherit the land. A little while, and the wicked will be no more; though you look for them, they will not be found. But the meek will inherit the land and enjoy great peace.

Getting caught up in the "rat race" of living is a common thing. People tend to run a competitive race against one another. It would seem the measure of achievement is seen in the physical world of possessions. How much you make, where you live, the car you drive, and where your kids go to school, are all things people use to measure achievement. The drive to achieve is the major force behind the "what" and the "why" of what people do.

The drive to achieve has many victims. Many people truly want to do the right thing, but just get caught up in the unrelenting drive to achieve, attain, and succeed.

The ones who don't end up as victims, do end up confused. The confusion robs them of a quality of life. They always desire more. They want to live comfortably, but don't want to sell out to the treacherous and compromising ways of a materialistic world.

Learning how to strike a balance and live within some reasonable perimeters is the key to success, happiness, and holiness. This balance is hard to achieve because most of the time we don't make the issues clear enough to focus upon one practical, application principle.

The drive to achieve is not bad in (and of) itself. The drive must be directed and harnessed to maximize both your human potential in this life and your eternal destiny in the next. Achievement has the potential of building eternal qualities into your soul or consuming you with the addiction to achieve, possess, gain, and own. The addiction to achieve can consequently destroy the greatness of the soul.

Balancing lifestyle is never a quick job. Balance requires growth and patience. The growth actually comes from the patience.

Every state in America has an entire governmental department dedicated to the balancing of official scales.

Their people are carefully trained and carry a great deal of authority. Every roadway has limitations of height and weight. These limitations vary some from state to state. These state departments exist to provide safe and secure road passage. When big trucks pull up on the weigh scale they have to have a precise measurement because an overweight rig can receive heavy fines and be denied passage on the state's roadway. States want to prevent major accidents, erosion of their roadways, and over all balance of their systems. Keeping things balanced is essential in providing stability.

Balancing achievement in your personal life is essential. Everything you do, say, think, and experience comes into your life to be processed by the brain center. Combining all the endless input your brain receives requires a certain amount of concentration to keep it all balanced. The greatest attribute you can develop to help in the processing of all your input, is patience. Everyone needs patience to develop a balance in the area of achievement. By deciding to balance achievement, you have already decided to build patience into your life.

> **PATIENCE WILL HELP YOU BALANCE SUCCESS AND ACHIEVEMENT IF YOU APPLY IMPORTANT PRINCIPLES IN YOUR LIFE.**

#1 DON'T COMPARE YOURSELF TO OTHERS

"Keeping up with the Jones" is the old phrase that represents the idea of comparisons. It is the idea based upon keeping a lookout on what your neighbors have and keeping up with their lifestyle, possessions, caliber of vocation, etc. Coveting starts as simple comparison. Comparison becomes longing; longing becomes jealousy; and jealousy becomes covetousness.

In many arenas, the idea of comparisons is encouraged. In sales occupations, competition is the name of the game. Out doing the competition is often the difference in one's career advancement. On the outside we often succumb to this kind of pressure. It even feels right. In the short term it provides us with success, achievement, and security. But the long term effect of comparison, competition, and success are serious mental and emotional problems for many who have lost a balance when it comes to achievement.

Another problem with comparison is the tendency many people have to become dishonest. The pressure of reporting the number, chart, graph, or record brings with it the desire not to be embarrassed or out done by someone else. Many resort to dishonesty to avoid rejection in any form. Dishonesty carries with it a different kind of baggage that destroys people. Once you allow yourself to not tell the truth, you are opening up the door to degenerating all the levels of your integrity.

Some even resort to stealing to keep up with others. Over extending on credit is a form of stealing. If you put something on a credit card that you have no idea how you are going to pay for it, you are stealing from someone in the process. Of course we have all kinds of justification for borrowing, but no really good reason. It comes down to wanting something now. Developing the patience to wait is the only way to overcome the problem of comparison.

The "eyes of comparison" will continually get us into trouble at some level. The only way to live free from comparison is to develop patience in your life. Avoid comparing yourself to anyone else by determining to blaze your own path and leave a trail. Do what is best for you and your family to live a balanced life. When you begin to notice your life is not in balance, take immediate measures to balance things out again. Achievement is not a standardized measure. Life is not standard. No two people are the same. Life is individualized, not standardized. Don't allow yourself to become standardized by comparing yourself to others.

#2: EVERYTHING IN LIFE COMES AND GOES IN IT'S SEASON

God was the one who created seasons. Some seasons are intense, others mild. We can never fully pinpoint when the change of seasons will occur, but we know eventually the seasons will change.

Intense situations are like the intensity often seen in many weather changes. Intensity can cause life to go out of balance. The best way out of an adverse situation is often to endure the situation. By enduring an adverse situation you begin to realize that everything passes. This will help you become a stronger (and more patient) person.

When faced with difficult circumstances, remind yourself "this too will pass."

Physical or emotional pain often causes us to lose our balance. When going through pain the one thing we usually forget is "this too will pass." Often pain makes it feel like there will be no tomorrow. Preparation for painful experiences is overlooked. If we could firmly and fully realize that all things pass, that all things go in cycles, then we will be able to develop a better attitude during tough times.

The seasons of life teach us to lead better lives. We need to learn from the seasons and make application to situations more difficult later on. A good roof protects against the storms. Keeping your oil changed prevents having to scurry about when facing a possible trip. Oiling moving parts keeps them from freezing up. The ultimate maintenance to keeping the balance of achievement is to allow patience to grow through all of life's seasons.

#3: FIND YOUR REFUGE/SECURITY IN THE LORD

No one who runs away and hides ever feels very safe. That nagging sense of being found is always present. There are all kinds of hiding places, but not many safe ones. People are looking for safe places to land. Most of the time the place people land while trying to find a place of safety is short-term and dangerous.

Finding the right kind of "refuge" or place of security is difficult unless you reach an important conclusion: the refuge you need is already within you. The place of security and refuge in life is built upon a personal relationship with God.

God is not some elderly gentleman out there in the great beyond watching us for amusement. He is a creative genius wanting us to develop and reach our potential through growth in the inner life. It is in the inner life that God dwells. Developing the inner life through a personal relationship with God is like building a mighty fortress.

This inner fortress can only be built as you apply four things.

   ❑ **Trust the Lord completely with every area of your life.** Fully and positively realize everything in life comes from God. Thankfulness in the face of every situation is the proof of this.

- **Do good things.** Doing good leaves your conscience clear. Kindness sheds all forms of guilt.
- **Consider your relationship with the Lord to be a permanent one.** The concept of permanence will give you a feeling of security nothing else can give.
- **Be joyful.** Joy is the ultimate place of refuge because it protects us emotionally and mentally from all harm. As people learn the meaning of enjoyment, they can turn their meaningless or pointless lives completely around. Enjoyment of life is a process, not an event.

#4: BE FLEXIBLE WHILE GOD IS WORKING IN YOUR LIFE

Patience is developed in life as we accept everything that comes our way as God working in our lives. As this attitude is developed, a calm and peaceful acceptance of every circumstance in life will come over you.

Become flexible, soft and pliable rather than hard, cold and stubborn; then you will be able to keep the balance in all achievement.

People who are hard-nosed have too much pride. God's intent is to purge our lives of pride. The only way for this to happen is to be softened. People with pride expect God to always change His mind and will to accommodate them. The person who is soft and pliable is able to change personal demands and come into submission to God's will.

#5: STAY COMMITED TO A CENTRAL FOCUS

Businesses are continually striving to be more productive. They urge management to define a company's purpose. To achieve this goal, the question constantly arises--"Why are we doing this?" In answering that question, a company is able to define its purpose. Personally, defining a purpose helps us do something more important--and that is to narrow our focus.

Focus is critical to balancing achievement in your life. If you don't maintain a certain level of focus, you will generally live unbalanced.

Eyeglasses, telescopes, microscopes, magnifying glasses, and cameras all have to do with focus. Without focus, life is just a blur. You have to be able to see clearly to achieve.

When taking pictures, many cameras have automatic focus. The focus in a picture depends upon depth, angle, and how many people in a picture. Developing good focus personally is not unlike taking a picture. Determine your commitment, and then adjust your intensity to that commitment. In doing this, you generally redefine your priorities. This helps in improving your focus.

There are great benefits to being a focussed person. One good way being focussed helps is preventing being "spread too thin." When you are "spread too thin," quality time is not given to tasks at hand. Things are rushed, and many times jobs break down. By being a focussed person, you are able to center in on the task at hand and do it well.

Burnout is the result of not focussing enough and, as a result, becoming worn out (physically and mentally exhausted). Many people are troubled and plagued by burnout. They have worked too hard and allowed their lives to get out of balance. They have taken themselves way too seriously, and now their achievement is out of balance. Developing focus will help to change burnout.

#6: EXECUTE HOLDING PATTERNS IN YOUR LIFE

Holding patterns in life are inevitable. How we handle the holding patterns in life determines our ability to stay balanced. We usually interpret patience and waiting as sitting back and taking it easy. Nothing could be further from the truth. Patience requires great concentration. Waiting requires discipline. Concentration and discipline are essential for creating nurture in your inner life, for those times when things in life are on "hold."

Airplanes are placed in holding patterns if the weather conditions are too poor to land, or the airport is too busy, or other airplanes are trying to land. Each airplane is prioritized and given a number. The planes circle an assigned pattern before given permission to land.

Holding patterns are important because they prevent collisions, crashes, and even death. Although they require patience, every holding pattern is good for you.

Waiting, in any context, never has to be a negative experience. During times of waiting you can determine to build and grow in your inner life. Let the wait build your character. Let the holding pattern make you grow.

Embracing holding patterns may be opposite to the point of view of many sales organizations, but it is the right point of view! Developing growth during holding patterns will help balance achievement. By developing this concept of holding patterns, much of the worry and tension of day to day living can be managed easier. Learning the holding patterns of different arenas of life will give the sense of purpose and well being. You know that you have done all you can do and still retain a clear conscience. Holding patterns are a gift from God. Thank Him for them the next time you are in a holding pattern.

#7: DON'T LET YOURSELF GET WORKED UP

Channeling emotions is how many people are trained to succeed and achieve. Emotion allowed to go out of control is never a good idea. The wider the swings of emotion, the wider they will continue to grow. If you don't consistently manage your emotions, your emotions will manage you!

Success and achievement can cause your emotions to go out of control easily. There are very few people who don't get worked up about things occasionally. Whenever your emotions are out of control--you are out of control. This will always cause life to go out of balance for a while. Depending on the swing of emotion, it can take quite a while to get life back into balance after emotion has taken control.

When people are worked up they often say and do unpredictable things. During these times things can get pretty rough, especially if someone else is involved. Some of the biggest mistakes ever made occur during these times. Out of control emotion cause people to think wrongly. When we think wrongly, we act wrongly.

People who learn not to get worked up are generally people with a great peace in their lives. These are people who are balanced in the area of achievement, patient in their inner life, and don't mind waiting upon the Lord.

FOR SITUATIONS THAT ARE TENSE:

Proverbs 15:18 A hot-tempered man stirs up dissension, but a patient man calms a quarrel.

FOR SITUATIONS NEEDING AN IMMEDIATE ANSWER:

Ecclesiastes 7:8-9 The end of a matter is better than its beginning, and patience is better than pride. Do not be quickly provoked in your spirit, for anger resides in the lap of fools.

FOR SITUATIONS WHERE YOU NEED A CALM HEAD:

Luke 21:19 By standing firm you will gain life.

FOR SITUATIONS WHEN YOU ARE IN A HOLDING PATTERN:

2 Peter 1:5-8 For this very reason, make every effort to add to your faith goodness; and to goodness, knowledge; and to knowledge, self-control; and to self-control, perseverance; and to perseverance, godliness; and to godliness, brotherly kindness; and to brotherly kindness, love. For if you possess these qualities in increasing measure, they will keep you from being ineffective and unproductive in your knowledge of our Lord Jesus Christ.

FOR SITUATIONS WHEN YOU ARE ABOUT TO COMPLAIN:

Exodus 16:12   "I have heard the grumbling of the Israelites. Tell them, 'At twilight you will eat meat, and in the morning you will be filled with bread. Then you will know that I am the LORD your God."

CHAPTER 3: TAMING THE BEAST WITH PATIENCE

1 Thessalonians 5:14 Now we exhort you, brethren...be patient toward all men.

Ephesians 4:2 Be patient bearing with one another in love.

A lack of patience not only causes difficulties in personal and professional lives, but also in our internal lives. A lack of patience internally can create a whole world of problems that hide just below the surface of all relationships and situations.

Hiding below the surface of most situational and relationship problems is anger.

People with problems in their personal lives can trace it back to some kind of unresolved anger. When we think of anger, we picture our parents blowing their stack because we were bad. Worse yet, we picture abuse, brutality, and even murder.

Actually, anger is a word that denotes the rage within from some unresolved conflict. Those who don't resolve their inner conflicts experience anger. These people are from all walks of life. They are addictive, abusive, argumentative, competitive, or codependent. Additionally, there is an another entire world of the angry. The world of the angry is comprised of those people who don't resolve conflict, but don't exhibit their anger in external ways. Anger in these people is a silent killer. Because they haven't dealt with their conflicts and they mask their anger, they are internalizing anger into their physical and mental systems. These people end up with various levels of physical and mental problems directly correlated to their anger.

Story after story could be told of people with unresolved anger. The problem is multiplied when people with unresolved anger have children. Because they have never dealt with their anger, the anger is passed on to their children through countless emotional/mental ways. Generation after generation of people can be filled with different forms of anger because conflicts are not resolved.

It does not have to be this way! Conflicts can be resolved and anger can be managed. Taming the beast of anger through patience requires two very important things--identification and resolution. These two things can change the entire direction of a life. There are five basic areas of anger identification. When you identify an area in your life--don't panic! Anger is manageable. Conflicts are resolvable. However, it requires work and patience.

In each identifying mark of anger is an equally important resolve. If you put the work into the resolve, you will be able to manage the element you identify. Don't do one without the other. It won't do you any good to identify anger if you are not interested in resolving it.

In the same way, it won't do you any good to try to resolve something you won't freely admit is present in your life. Each of these points requires patience. Patience is the only thing that will help you tame the beast of anger!

A PERSON WITH UNRESOLVED ANGER CREATES TENSION--TENSION IS RESOLVED THROUGH PATIENT DEVELOPMENT OF POSITIVE COMMUNICATION.

An angry person creates tension wherever they go. Wherever you feel tension, anger is present. Tension is that underlying feeling that something is not quite right, but not dealt with either. Most angry people know (there are exceptions to this) they can't go around blowing their stack all the time at everyone. By holding it in, they act unnaturally, speak differently, and feel like a fake.

Tension brings with it strife, discontent, confusion, and non-confrontation. Tension generally puts everyone around it on the edge. This feeling can occur anywhere: at home, work, school, and even at church. Many times a day people will remark--"boy, you could sure feel the tension."

The only way to resolve tension is through communication. Clearing the air and talking things through relieves most of the difficulty in tension. Angry people communicate their anger. The resolve of their anger has to start somewhere. Sharing their feelings can be difficult for both the angry person and the people around them. It is hard for an angry person to communicate because they haven't had any role models to follow. People around them find it hard to listen to an angry person who is starting to communicate because an angry person is also a blamer. Angry people will blame all of their problems on to people who will take it.

It is essential that communication have ground rules. Trust, love, and support are key elements in learning to communicate. Communication should begin as kindly as possible.

> **A PERSON WITH UNRESOLVED ANGER CAN NEVER ADMIT TO A MISTAKE--THIS KIND OF PRIDE IS RESOLVED THROUGH THE PATIENT DEVELOPMENT OF HUMILITY.**

Angry people are proud people. The pride is actually a defensive mechanism developed subconsciously by the psyche to protect itself against attack. Angry people feel they have been so attacked that they would never admit to any kind of failure, lest they be attacked again.

An interesting irony is angry people make a lot of mistakes. Pride alone creates an atmosphere where perfection is always demanded. No one can live this way very long without realizing he/she can never live up to perfectionism. Instead of admitting this as truth, an angry person goes on trying to convince himself/herself that they are living up to their perfectionist life.

Pride induces insecurity that creates defensiveness. Whenever you see pride, insecurity, and defensiveness, you will see mistakes. These mistakes are never admitted to, so the cycle continues to degenerate on and on.

The way to resolve this kind of problem is through humility. Humility is the simple internalization that no one is perfect--not even you! Don't take things so seriously. In life you never have to be perfect about/with anything. All you need is an attitude of growth. Grow from all the events of life. Learn to laugh at yourself. Accept yourself. Accept others and they will readily accept you.

A PERSON WITH UNRESOLVED ANGER IS POSSESSIVE--POSSESSIVENESS IS RESOLVED THROUGH THE PATIENT DEVELOPMENT OF PASSION.

Anger is passion. This identifying area of anger should be an easy one to resolve since it takes the same kind of energy to be passionate as it does to be angry.

An angry person is possessive. Possessiveness can be observed in a person as jealousy, deep-seeded materialistic patterns, or addictions. Possessive people are so insecure they want to control and dominate everything in their life. They are rarely satisfied with a small part, but feel the need to take over. When they sense resistance to their need to dominate, they will begin subtle approaches through manipulation.

Possessiveness can be changed using the same kind of energy that it exhibits. The possessive energy is the passionate kind. If every person who is possessive of life could look inward, he could actually change his own possessiveness to passion. Passion is simply that energy level that creates an atmosphere of emotion. At that point, the choice of whether it is positive emotion or negative emotion is up to the individual.

Becoming passionate has some predictable side effects. A passionate person will often go overboard. Passionate people have a certain amount of mood swings. Sometimes they will say things others disagree with. Sometimes the drives are insurmountable. These side effects of passion are all manageable if developing patience is the goal.

Turn Your Possessiveness
Into Passion
Through
Developing Patience.

The most feared evidence of anger is violence. Everyone knows someone with this potential. These people deal with their anger on an external basis. Many times when these people hit a certain point, they don't care who is around when they explode. Sometimes they blank out and don't even remember going off.

Because people like this have such deep feelings of anger, they often feed their own impulses by blaming others. It is always someone else's fault. By blaming others, they can justify their violent behavior.

The only way to effectively deal with this kind of anger is spiritually. Godliness is a term that is the total picture of the Gospel. Godliness means the birth of Jesus by a virgin, his death on the cross, burial, resurrection from the dead, the ascension to the right hand of the Father--and--my participation in propagating this teaching.

Violent anger must be totally emptied out of a person's life. The emptiness left behind has to be filled up with something--which is why Godliness as a new lifestyle makes sense.

A PERSON WITH UNRESOLVED ANGER IS A NEGATIVE & COMPLAINING PERSON-- NEGATIVITY IS RESOLVED THROUGH THE PATIENT DEVELOPMENT OF THANKFULNESS.

Anger is always present in the life of a negative person. A negative person criticizes, whines, complains, or scrutinizes others. These are insecure people who have never dealt with conflicts in their own lives. They feel better about themselves by putting others down.

It is anger within a person that causes them to nit-pick at weaknesses or idiosyncrasies in others. People nit-pick at weaknesses in others that they exhibit in their own lives. Those who complain and murmur think they are hiding their real problem. The truth is, they are exposing the real problem, not hiding it. Their own anger raises its ugly head.

The way to resolve the anger that comes from being negative is to become thankful. Take a daily inventory of all the things you are thankful for and think about them. Developing a thankful attitude is as simple as any choice you would make. You choose to be thankful or negative at each point along the way. A negative person becomes more angry. A positive person becomes more patient.

❑ **"Do all things without murmurings and disputings." Philippians 2:14**

Unresolved conflict is a silent killer because it creeps up through anger. Anger is a beast that kills from the inside out. It consumes, tortures, and then kills a soul.

Anger is resolvable. **The beast can be tamed through patience!** Readily identify these five qualities of anger and put into practice.

❑ **Colossians 3:12-15 Therefore, as God's chosen people, holy and dearly loved, clothe yourselves with compassion, kindness, humility, gentleness and patience. Bear with each other and forgive whatever grievances you may have against one another. Forgive as the Lord forgave you. And over all these virtues put on love, which binds them all together in perfect unity. Let the peace of Christ rule in your hearts, since as members of one body you were called to peace. And be thankful.**

CHAPTER 4: DEVELOPING PATIENCE WITH PEOPLE

The hardest kind of patience to develop is patience toward others. Exhibiting patience toward people is the greatest test of character.

Whether it is an ongoing agitation of a neighbor, the messy room of a child, or the slowness of a store clerk, human relationships require patience.

Several years ago there was a man outside washing a new company truck. He worked for a local utility and took a truck home each night. Every ten years or so their trucks got replaced. It was obvious how much pride the man had in this new prize. He painstakingly went over every square inch with his sponge. Sometime during the drying off of the truck, his four-year-old son came rolling out of the garage on his little bicycle. This normal four-year-old scooted over to his father for some attention. The father stayed focussed on the truck without acknowledging the little boy. The boy pulled his bike beside the truck and leaned against it holding himself up with his hand. "YOU GET AWAY FROM MY TRUCK--NOW!" The words exploded out of the father to the son. The young boy's head bowed and body shrunk. It was a deep response of embarrassment. The father's message was loud and clear--the truck was more important at that moment than the boy. The father was making it clear through his words and attitude what his priorities were.

This kind of situation is repeated time and again. We seem to have more affection, affirmation, and patience for a material possession than we do each other. It is sad to think we treat things better than we do others. Often times we love things and use people rather than love people and use things. The more affection we have for material possessions, the less likely we are to have patience with people.

Developing patience with people requires some work. The application of some key principles is essential to develop the necessary patience with people to achieve any level of success in the world. Apply these concepts a little at a time at first. Realize how you treat others, and accept the responsibility for what you say and how you treat them. Next, apply a concept or two at a time until it becomes a part of your life. The harder you work to develop patience with people, the happier your life will be!

> **THE FIRST STEP TO DEVELOPING PATIENCE TOWARD PEOPLE IS TO BECOME MORE LENIENT TOWARD OTHERS IN YOUR ATTITUDE!**

Leniency is an often-ignored idea of our culture. Leniency requires us to think of others more than self. Since the defining characteristic of our culture is selfishness, it should not be a surprise that leniency is often missing. Introducing leniency to our culture would initially seem like bringing together two directly opposing concepts. It is important to introduce leniency because patience can be developed toward others, and because there are three practical keys to become more lenient.

❑ **Make excuses for people.** Making excuses for others aids us in excusing them from things that make us more impatient. Most of the things that upset us about others are things we could never do anything about anyway. Rather than get yourself worked up about things that you can't do anything about, let it go by excusing them. Making excuses for others in your own mind will change how you view others. Your view of others is the major part of your patience problem.

❑ **Disregard all forms of negative things.** There is bad in the best person and good in the worst person, what you look for in another person is exactly what you will find. The reason you see so many negatives with others is because that is what you are looking for in them. We need to emphasize the positive in others and disregard the negative. Doing this helps us not to be too picky or critical. It also helps us set the pace to be more understanding of others.

❑ **Empathize.** Empathy is to put yourself in the "shoes" of someone else. This is really the ultimate kind of human understanding. To show empathy, you have to be empty of your own selfishness. When this happens, leniency can truly come full circle in your life.

THE SECOND STEP TO DEVELOPING PATIENCE TOWARD OTHERS IS TO AVOID GRUMBLING ABOUT OTHERS!

Grumbling about others has some very negative implications. It generates a negative atmosphere that lends itself to a self-gratifying, self-centered attitude. The more you grumble about others--the more impatient you will become toward them because of how selfish you are becoming.

Grumbling about the mistreatment you received will actually set yourself up for more mistreatment. A person who is victimized is often the victim of repeated unfortunate circumstances because they fall into a victim's mentality. A grumbling mentality positions itself for more mistreatment.

Grumbling about bad service you received works the same way. The more you grumble, the more you will affect your own attitude. The more you see bad service, the worse you will be treated by people wanting to serve you because of the type of treatment you will give them.

Your own negative attitude will affect others--which affects you in return.

Grumbling works you up. Other people won't come right out and admit it, but they won't want to be around you.

Grumbling creates a negative atmosphere all the way around. This kind of atmosphere puts others on the edge. Because everyone is on the edge, those around you won't be able to get along. This kind of environment is not conducive to developing patience, but impatience. It can all be solved by not grumbling about others.

THE THIRD STEP TO DEVELOPING PATIENCE TOWARD OTHERS IS TO AVOID UNNECESSARY TALK.

Avoiding unnecessary talk is not to say "don't talk" but rather "don't talk so much." Unnecessary talk has a tendency to create friction, misunderstanding, disputes, conflict, fantasy, and even vulgarity. Unnecessary talk creates an atmosphere for too close relationships where the wrong people know too much. Unnecessary talk also brings alienation of those who need to get along, but can't because of unnecessary dialogue.

Practicing restraint with the things you say will help you in all areas of your life. The discipline you will train yourself in will help you to became a more mature, patient person.

This concept can be easily summed up in the old adage--"better to be thought a fool than open one's mouth and remove all doubt."

> ## THE FOURTH STEP TO DEVELOPING PATIENCE TOWARD OTHERS IS TO REALIZE THERE ARE SOME PEOPLE YOU WILL JUST HAVE TO DECIDE TO TOLERATE.

There will always be people who are hard to get along with. The type of person hard to tolerate varies with individual personalities. To tolerate them, realize God has placed them in our lives for a reason. God intends for us to grow and build character through our relationships. Growth happens faster when faced with adverse conditions.

Many times a day people are faced with dealing with people they don't care for. Some people are forced into these situations at work. These situations can often go on for years. When conditions go on for a long period of time, a choice is made as to whether patience or impatience will develop.

There are three things anyone can do when faced with having to tolerate people who are not tolerable. This will work in any context of personality conflict.

❑ **Don't antagonize.** Don't work things up. Don't stir things up. Let the dust settle on issues. Hope for the best. Antagonizing a person or situation creates friction far beyond just you and another person. Seek for peace, not friction in relationships.

❑ **Don't try to change someone else.** A very common mistake is thinking you can change someone. The only person you can change is you. If you change your own attitude, you are able to change an entire situation.

❑ **Don't let people who are hard for you to tolerate occupy your thoughts.** If you allow a situation to occupy your thoughts, you will end up making the outcome much worse. It will wear you down. When you are worn down, you will do and say things making the situation much worse.

THE FIFTH STEP TO DEVELOPING PATIENCE TOWARD OTHERS IS TO BE QUICK TO FORGIVE.

Forgiveness is what love is really all about. People who develop the ability to forgive quickly, will create for themselves a whole world of love. Forgiveness is a unique miracle that lies within each of us. If we choose to forgive, we can change our lives. Change is as quick as forgiveness.

45

Forgiveness can happen if you decide to pardon others. Pardoning people who offend you will put your whole life in a new perspective.

Forgiveness can happen if you decide to let go of what people say to you. Letting go of things said can be a challenge to people who are insecure. It is also hard for people who fear the rejection of others to let go. You have to let go if you are going to develop patience toward others. If you don't let go, you will always be paranoid concerning what people say or think.

Forgiveness can happen if you lend people a hand. Help other people out on a regular basis. Don't wait for them to ask. Helping people out will help you see what they go through. By getting your eyes off yourself, you will be able to forgive people easier.

Invest yourself in people. Do someone a favor once in a while. If you help someone you don't like, it will help you see him/her, and yourself, in a different way. This will help you create a new outlook that will facilitate the development of patience with people.

THE SIXTH STEP TO DEVELOPING PATIENCE TOWARD OTHERS IS TO MAKE THE SIMPLE DETERMINATION THAT YOU ARE GOING TO BE MORE PATIENT TOWARD THEM.

Good old determination can prove to be one of your most effective tools in becoming more patient with others. From time to time, you will find the only way to deal with someone is shear endurance. Allow those times to become character builders. Grow and become strong during those times of difficulty in relationships. Above all things, let those times of difficulty find you to be patient with others.

Making the determination to mature and become patient in the face of all circumstances, will make every circumstance in your life worth something. **Every circumstance is a character builder!**

CHAPTER 5: TRAINING YOURSELF TO TAKE THINGS LIGHTER

Proverbs 15:13--"A happy heart makes the face cheerful, but heartache crushes the spirit."

Proverbs 15:15--"All the days of the oppressed are wretched, but the cheerful heart has a continual feast."

In years past, people were more concerned about survival than their health. Foods we consider unhealthy today were not only consumed, they were accepted with great appreciation. Bacon and eggs cooked in lard, toast with real butter, cups of real cream, and plenty of coffee provided people with a decent breakfast.

Today we read the side of every box to examine the ingredients. Words like fat, sugar, protein, carbohydrate, relate to words like hypertension, heart disease, obesity, and diabetes. The more educated we become, the more attention is given to a long and healthy life. The more we study, the more we see how diet has to do with sickness and disease.

This new information has required the food industry to produce items more in line with a healthier lifestyle. Now that society has changed, we are seeing food that is "cholesterol free," "fat free," "low calorie," or even "lite." We have wised up and become "lighter."

At the same time, this same society that has wised up and decided to eat healthier and exercise, lives more stressed out emotionally/mentally than ever before. Stress and pressure on people in their daily lives is greater than ever. Life is fast-paced, with a "win at any cost" and "drive-thru" mentality. The life many people lead is in stark contrast to the new, healthy emphasis in our culture, including eating right and exercising.

No matter how healthy people eat, or how regularly they exercise, they still will die prematurely if they can't manage stress.

Doctors tell us that attitude has as much to do with developing or overcoming cancer as diet does. There is a bumper sticker that reads "Eat well--Stay fit--Die anyway." As sarcastic as this bumper sticker is, there is some truth in it. People work out, run, and bike to get into shape and to stay fit. They eat right and count calories. At the same time, they may be neglecting an area of true health--**the inner life**. A person may have the perfect body, but if the mind is stressed, something needs to change.

We need to learn to become "lite" on the inside-- not intellectually or in intelligence, but on the stress level.

The only way to achieve becoming "lite" is by realizing the importance of patience in your life. People who develop patience live under much less stress and pressure than impatient people. Developing the kind of life with less stress and more patience can be achieved as you **train yourself to become lighter in your inner life**.

A lighter life is within the reach of anyone who desires it. A lighter mind will purge the thought, feeling, and emotion from tensions that can cause disease, unrest, and overall edginess.

> ## TRAIN YOURSELF TO BECOME "LITE"(LIGHTER) AND YOU WILL BECOME FREE FROM THE KIND OF STRESS AND PRESSURE THAT CAUSE SICKNESS AND DISEASE!

Train yourself to not take yourself so seriously. We all have a tendency to take ourselves too seriously. The typical response to disappointment is defensiveness followed by anger. People become angry to avoid depression. This cycle always makes matters much worse.

We have to train ourselves to understand that it doesn't really matter that we win all the time. It doesn't really matter if we ever win at all. It is important to come to the conclusion that you have been taking things too seriously, and the time has come to break yourself of this bad habit.

The best way to break the habit of taking yourself too seriously is to be more conscious of those times you feel yourself becoming intense, competitive, or serious over issues. Once you have taken the step of becoming more conscious about matters you take too seriously, the next step is a decision. You need to make the decision to let it go. Whatever is making you intense--you must let it go.

People who take things too seriously pay for this habit through the break down of their health. The stress of their own intensity attacks the weakest part of their body. Deciding to "let it go" should be an easy decision to make if you realize your health is at stake!

Learn to let things go easily. Most of things that get us intense won't matter one bit a day from now, or a week from now, or a year from now. Everything that works you up will eventually work out--on its own. The only thing your intensity affects is you (and your health).

No person is the main spoke of the wheel. Everything does not depend on one person. People who think "it all depends on me" have put their ego ahead of the facts. Anything truly worth while is put together over the course of time, with the help and ownership of many people.

Train yourself to stop worrying. Better than 95% of the things people worry about never come to pass. Worry has a way of making things seem much larger than they are.

There is a big difference between a healthy concern and worry. Being concerned about something keeps us focussed and on task. Worry is a preoccupation. People prone to worry never really have any peace. When the things people worry about don't come to pass, they just create new things to worry about.

Worry zaps your energy. The energy worry consumes could be invested in many other more positive ways. You can train yourself to stop worrying and make your life lighter by applying three simple steps.

- ❑ **Don't worry about things you don't have any control over.** If you can't do anything about it--don't think about it. Let it go. When you find yourself worrying, this should be the first thing you ask yourself--"Do I have any control over the outcome?" If the answer is "no," you should dismiss the whole thing from your mind.
- ❑ **Do your best, then forget about it.** Work hard, do your best, then forget it. There is nothing you can do to help anything if it is after the fact. Many of the things we worry about are after the fact. If you are worrying about something before the fact, use the

energy you are wasting to do something about it--then forget it!

❑ **Visualize worry as your enemy.** See worry as a sickness or disease you are trying to avoid. Don't let it come even close to you. Don't spend time around others who are consumed in their worry.

Train yourself to set priorities. Edginess and intensity can develop when there are too many things to do and not enough time to do it in. When there are too many things to do, you don't have direction and end up spinning your wheels and becoming frustrated.

To prevent having too many things to do, it is important to set your priorities on every occasion. Learn to know what is the most important and what is the least important. Know how to prioritize your life on all the things in between the most and least important.

When faced with unsettling circumstances, remind yourself of the priorities you set. If you don't have them in place, set up your priorities on the spot in your mind. Go after the top thing on the priority list--do your best-- then let it go to move on to the next one. Even if you don't ever get finished with the first thing, at least you tried. Trying is good enough! The goal is to develop patience by lightening up your life. It is not to do everything on your priority list.

Train yourself to keep a good perspective. Perspective is how you see things. It is how good your focus is on certain things. But, it also includes the ability to automatically focus. When things get too close, heat up too much, or become too intense, your focussing lens automatically takes a step or two back to regain the focus.

Perspective is something we must constantly adjust. Without a proper perspective, we will always see things wrong.

Whenever you feel like your schedule is getting out of hand, immediately take a break from things and take a deep breath. A momentary break can do much to regain perspective. Learn to identify the need for a new perspective in yourself.

Train yourself to not do everything today. You always have tomorrow to finish things up. You don't have to get all your work done in one day. Quotas, goals, assignments, and requirements have become the great stress builder of our day.

Learn to do your best every day--one day at a time. Then the load you carry will be much lighter.

Impatience increases when you put yourself and others under a load of pressure trying to do more, be more, or sell more. If you live under this kind of stress, patience will never be given an opportunity to develop.

Train yourself to not be a slave to your schedule. Freeing yourself up from a schedule might not be possible. If it is not, make sure you have periods of time daily, weekly, and annually that you are not bound to any schedule.

If we were totally honest with ourselves, we would find that much of the schedule bondage we are under is self-induced. We try to blame this or that, but the schedule we keep is our own making. Honestly analyze your own schedule. Do you have times that are free in your schedule? If not, you are doing too much.

We convince ourselves we need a certain kind of job, a certain income, and a certain lifestyle because it is important. Who is it all really important to? In many cases, life could be so much happier for people who would lower their standard of living, reduce their debt load, change careers (or at least a job), and live with less stress.

The inner life has a greater capacity to sustain you than your material life. A person with patience not only lives longer, lives healthier, and lives freer, but also <u>lives better!</u>

<u>Train yourself to laugh</u>. Laugh hard and laugh often. Don't laugh at others, laugh at yourself. Don't laugh "at"--laugh "with."

Laughter is the greatest kind of medicine. It relaxes the body and relieves the soul. Look for things to make you laugh. Chuckle to yourself often. Smile a lot. Smile at people. It will immediately begin to lift your own spirits.

Laughter has often been overlooked. Situation comedy is a popular primetime evening entertainment. People watch sit-coms because they can relate to what is going on in the program. People are also desperate to laugh. Everyone knows how good it feels to laugh--we just have to start!

"LIGHTEN" UP YOUR LIFE:

❑ **Don't take yourself so seriously.**

❑ **Stop worrying.**

❑ **Set priorities.**

❑ **Keep a good perspective.**

❑ **Don't do everything in one day.**

❑ **Don't be a slave to a schedule.**

❑ **Laugh hard and laugh often.**

CHAPTER 6: PATIENCE AT WORK IN LIFESTYLE

Proverbs 30:8 Keep falsehood and lies far from me; give me neither poverty nor riches, but give me only my daily bread.

Ecclesiastes 2:24 A man can do nothing better than to eat and drink and find satisfaction in his work. This too, I see, is from the hand of God.

Ecclesiastes 4:6 Better one handful with tranquillity than two handfuls with toil and chasing after the wind.

1 Timothy 6:8-11 But if we have food and clothing, we will be content with that. People who want to get rich fall into temptation and a trap and into many foolish and harmful desires that plunge men into ruin and destruction. For the love of money is a root of all kinds of evil. Some people, eager for money, have wandered from the faith and pierced themselves with many grieves. But you, man of God, flee from all this, and pursue righteousness, godliness, faith, love, endurance and gentleness.

Lifestyle encompasses all the areas of your life. Your family, your job, your home, your finances, and what you do with your leisure time, are all components of what makes up lifestyle. Patience at work in your lifestyle can mean the difference between success or failure at any level.

Finances

Everyone knows they need to save money. It is often not realized that patience in savings can mean the difference between success and failure. Most people get a little ahead financially, and then spend their savings on something. As patience grows, so does the ability to not buy something on an impulse.

Credit card buying is often the result of a lack of patience. Rather than saving up to buy something, it is much easier to buy now and pay later. People run themselves into deep problems with debt because they have never learned to be patient in their lifestyle. Whether it is the need for new furniture, clothes for a job, or an instrument for the kids to learn to play, there are always ways to spend all of your money--and to spend money you don't have. Plan ahead for purchases. Save up the money before you make purchases, and pay with cash. More people are going bankrupt than ever before. Some people go bankrupt two and three times. They haven't taken the time to learn patience, and get caught in the same financial trap time and time again.

Career

People are changing careers more than ever before. It is easier to relocate and move for a job. Many are doing it. No one likes a lateral job move. Everyone wants to move on to the bigger and better. The truth is-- bigger is not always better. Careers are not something that grow overnight. Building your career requires plenty of patience. People who skip here, to there, and back again, are people who always think there is a deal out there they are missing. Patience is the key to your career. Career progress doesn't always happen as fast as you want, but don't lose heart. Every day you are on the job, you are learning something. Most importantly, you are learning something about yourself. The more you know about yourself, the better off you are. Patience grows as we mature and wait things out over the course of time. Moving and skipping around does not help your patience, it feeds your drive. There is always a day of reckoning for people looking for the bigger and better.

Family

Family issues round out the lifestyle area. There are so many dynamics in every family. Every one of these dynamics comes back to one thing that could bring success--patience. Patience with your loved ones, their lives, their loves, and their interests is the key to family success. Not everyone in a family is ever going to be on the same page at the same time. Most of the time we have the unreasonable expectation that the family is going to merrily and happily agree on everything all the time. Nothing could be further from what things are actually like in anyone's family. Family success is painfully hard. The only measure of success comes from those families willing to let patience grow in them.

Learn to be more patient with your family issues and you will start to see immediate changes. Everyone in a family needs space and time to process things. Not rushing each other will go a long way to building needed trust between people.

Patience can work in your lifestyle if you make application of three distinct dynamics. These three dynamics will go a long way in helping you develop patience and maturity in your lifestyle.

GODLINESS

Godliness has to come first if you are going to develop patience in your lifestyle. Understanding what Godliness means is important, but applying Godliness is critical. The understanding and application of Godliness can change your life.

The New Testament word in the original language for Godliness is EUSEBIA. This word refers to the entire gospel scheme. The word picture means the death, burial, resurrection, and ascension of Jesus to the right hand of the Father--AND--**MY PERSONAL INVOLVEMENT IN THE PROCLAMATION OF THIS STORY.** "Involvement" means the active and personal participation in telling people about the claims of Christ.

The essence of Godliness is not something you do, it is who you are.

Godliness is more than a term, a concept, or even a dynamic--it is a lifestyle. Godliness is the life of the Christian believer. If the application of Godliness becomes the life of the Christian believer, very few other things will matter at all. When this Godliness mentality occurs, patience is developing because the Christian believer turns those things that would cause stress, quickly and easily over to God.

Godliness is something we work at every day. The Godliness lifestyle becomes more important to us than the car we drive, the place we live, the clothes we wear, or our status in life. As the Gospel scheme becomes our most important issue, our view of the world changes.

Godliness doesn't mean we give up all the other things in our lifestyle. It does mean we have a different reason for doing the things we do. Wherever people are, the Gospel needs to go out. Fishing, boating, hunting, swimming, running errands, mall shopping, or athletics-- wherever people are--we need to use for the purpose of Godliness. If you accept this important challenge of using all activities for Godliness, it will change your whole world. It will also produce a depth of patience you have never experienced before.

CONTENTMENT

Contentment is often an elusive thing to those who get stuck between the drive to succeed and the guilt of thinking they are not grateful enough. The underlying miracle of contentment is in the calm assurance that everything will work out fine. In this way, the state of contentment should be easy to achieve. Any time you are feeling apprehensive or concerned, remind yourself that everything is going to work out fine. You might have to repeat the idea a few times or really concentrate on it, but contentment can work for you.

The assurance in contentment is the essence of faith. Faith is simply entrusting your concerns to someone or something beyond yourself. Faith really kicks in when times are tough. It is also during the tough times that you really are able to learn some things about yourself. In this way, failure is always a better teacher than success. This is true because people listen better during the times of failure. During the times of success, people always think they did everything right and don't really need to listen or learn.

Contentment is not carelessness or laziness. These negative qualities should not be confused with the positive aspects of contentment.

The more contentment one has, the more contentment one develops because of the building and growing aspect of faith.

Work is an area where contentment can be utilized to its full extent. Enjoy your work. Do what it takes to have and keep a job that is enjoyable to you. If you don't enjoy your work, all areas of your life will be miserable. No one is great at faking work satisfaction. It becomes impossible to "flip the switch" all the time between happiness and misery.

Work must be fulfilling. If your work is not fulfilling, you will never feel like your life makes a difference. One of the greatest need levels is the need to make a difference with your life.

Work must be kept in its proper place. A job is just a job. It serves a purpose, and it pays the bills. Your job is not who you are. A job should never be allowed to jeopardize your faith or your family. If it does, your job has too much power over you.

In old European prisons, if the walls fell in, the prisoners were allowed to go free because of the divine intervention. The proper idea of contentment can be paralleled at this point. If you were a prisoner, what would you do if you knew you could go free if the walls fell in? Wouldn't you strike a balance between putting some amount of pressure on the walls every day--but not bruise yourself up by banging into them all day long? Contentment does not mean we don't try the walls (knock on the doors), we just accept the outcomes of life and live within our means in the mean time.

Lifestyle contentment has to meet two criteria:
1) Your lifestyle honors God. 2) You have a clear conscience.

ATTITUDE ABOUT MONEY

God never intended for money to be the center of our world. God meant for our worship of Him to be the center of our economy. Instead, the center of our economy is pictures of dead Presidents.

Money is simply a means to an end--but we have made it an end in itself. Our personal attitude concerning money will affect every area of our lives. The more we make money a center of our lives, the more it becomes an idol. The bigger the issue money becomes, the greater our bondage and our impatience will become.

Personal response to money varies from person to person. Some think money is to spend. Some think money is to save. Some think money is just an idea--that the credit card is really the thing to use. Whatever your attitude is about money, it will affect every decision you make in your life. Since money is such a big issue, we need principles to guide us concerning its use.

God wants us to be blessed, but that is not to say He wants us to be rich. All through the Bible the idea of "gain" or even "great gain" refers to becoming all you can be--living up to your full potential. Accumulation and prosperity have something to do with this, but is not the center of it.

We can stay on track with our lifestyle especially relating to money. Patience can develop within our lives through our money resources if we apply several important principles.

1. **Put God first.** When we see God as our source, we are able to put Him first. Impatience is fed when we see our possessions--and especially our money--as "mine all mine." God has to be first with our money resources. When you receive any kind of increase, remember to give Him back the first portion. Don't wait until the bills are paid, or you go to the grocery store, before you give to God. If you put God first in your finances, you will always have enough.

2. **Live within your means**. Don't go into debt for something you should save up for. Be patient and save up for things you need. The more you do this, the easier managing money will be.

3. **Money is a means to an end--not an end in itself.** It is the product of services rendered. Learn to serve others. Let money be a product of your service.

4. **Don't put a price tag on everything.** Get your mind off money! Don't see everything through the eyes of money. Expand yourself. Go beyond how you have been conditioned.

Thinking only of money will destroy you and every relationship you have.

5. **Quit all forms of money fantasies.** Train yourself to enjoy what you presently have. Be thankful and express thankfulness for the things you have. Fantasies about money, wealth, and accumulation breeds discontent and impatience. If you think you need something new, don't buy it for a while. Clean up or fix up what you already have. Make things work longer. Take good care of the things you already have. Many of the things you think you can't live without, are things you don't even need!

> *MONITORING YOUR MONEY IS ONE OF THE MOST OBVIOUS FORMS OF MONITORING YOUR PATIENCE!*

CHANGE YOUR ATTITUDE ABOUT MONEY BY APPLYING THESE PRINCIPLES:

- Put God first.

- Live within your means.

- Money is a means to an end- not an end in itself.

- Don't put a price tag on everything.

- Quit all money fantasies.

CHAPTER 7: PATIENCE IN THE WORKPLACE

Ecclesiastes 5:12--"The sleep of the laborer is sweet, whether he eats little or much, but the abundance of a rich man permits him no sleep."

Work is as common as life itself. It takes up a large portion of our time. Everyone has some kind of work in his/her life. The baby and toddler play and sleep all day. This is their work. Education for the young is preparing them for work. Adults participate in the work force. The older adults retire because of a life of work. Even the independently wealthy "work" at preserving their position of wealth.

Work is good. God created us to be productive. Productivity is what work is.

Work doesn't stop there. Instead of finding fulfillment in the satisfaction of productivity, many people fall into the depths of stress and pressure from their work. Attitude about work is as old as civilization itself. Some civilizations were free to be productive and live. Others were enslaved and forced into labor for others. Attitude in the face of each of these civilizations is also different. Historians say the Great Pyramids of Egypt were built over a twenty-year period. During this time, over 20,000 people worked every day on the project.

Through Egyptian hieroglyphics, we are able to tell that these thousands of men were actually singing while they worked on this project.

The opposite scenario has occurred in our society. Many people are so miserable with their jobs or careers, they have to force themselves to just get up in the mornings. Unhappiness in the workplace breeds discontent in all areas of life. Family life becomes miserable because people are miserable with their life's work. This attitude can become devastating. If a miserable person does not realize what causes them to feel miserable, he/she will often blame the wrong thing. When work is miserable, a spousal relationship can often suffer the consequences. Others on the job begin to meet emotional needs, and emotional bonding develops with people other than the spouse.

Because of the amount of time spent at work, people often spend more time with people who are not their family than they do their own family. These developing relationships can become confusing to a person under stress and pressure from a job. They confuse love for bonding, and time together at work is confused with family time. Many families have fallen apart because of work pressure, and the inability to identify and deal with it.

Patience in the work place has to do with an attitude concerning work. Attitude is not just one aspect of work success--it is really the only aspect of work success. We need a new attitude about work and how it fits into our world. We need this new attitude to develop a new perspective and better priorities. We need to allow patience to produce a better quality of work and a greater measure of work life. Work can be fun, fruitful, and functional.

There are several concepts that can change how you think about your work, and how you deal with it. These concepts are for those who truly care about their lives, and improving their quality of life. These concepts will not work for those who like to complain, and then go back to the way things were. The only thing that will really help you with work is developing patience. Trying to climb the ladder, getting in good with the boss, becoming a workaholic, doing everyone's job--will not get you ahead any faster. It may seem like it works for the short term, but in the long term all you have done is lose your self-respect, alienate your family, and miss out on the things that really count in your life.

WHATEVER YOUR WORK IS--IT SHOULD BRING YOU ENJOYMENT!

If your work is miserable, you will be miserable. If your work is enjoyable, you will be joyful. Don't spend your life being miserable. Find (and then keep) a job you enjoy. It does not make sense spending the best hours of the day, and the best years of your life, doing something you hate to do.

Many people are enslaved to a certain lifestyle and are convinced they have to work a certain job or kind of job in order to maintain the lifestyle. No lifestyle can bring you happiness in and of itself. If you don't enjoy your work, you won't be able to enjoy your life. Even if you are able to enjoy your life, your loved ones won't be able to enjoy life knowing the misery you put yourself through just to maintain the family lifestyle.

Sometimes careers are rushed or forced ahead because of impatience. A person goes into deep debt to buy a home, a car, a vacation, or a toy, and then has to work all kinds of over time hours to pay for it. The first level of misery comes when you don't have the time to enjoy the thing you bought because of all the time away from home. The second level of misery comes when you realize everything in life gets old. You are paying for something long after you have gotten your fun out of it.

People who don't enjoy what they do often spend a lot of money trying to enjoy their lives. It is their way of dealing with the stress of doing something that makes them miserable. This becomes a never-ending stress cycle. It is much better to find work you enjoy, even if it pays less.

> # WHATEVER YOUR WORK IS--IT SHOULD BRING FULFILLMENT!

If your work is not fulfilling, you will not be able to find fulfillment. The greatest need a person has in his/her life is the need to make a difference. If you feel like you are not making a difference in your work--no hobby or amount of diversions will take up the slack.

People who are not fulfilled in their work try desperately to find fulfillment in many areas of their lives, but are never able to. No one is ever too old to find something fulfilling. Go to school. Get training. Explore and find out what is fulfilling to you. Don't go through your life feeling empty and incomplete.

Patiently look for what fulfills you. Patiently train for that career. Patiently find your fulfillment in that field of work.

WHATEVER YOUR WORK IS-- REMIND YOURSELF THAT WHEN IT ALL COMES DOWN TO IT--A JOB IS JUST A JOB!

Don't ever let your job become your entire life. Family, friends, and faith are all much more important than a job. Don't let yourself become a slave to your work. When it all comes down--faith, family, and few friends are all any of us has that last. Work is just temporary. (A job is just a job).

Climbing the corporation ladder can be compared to the number of children who play basketball and want to play in the NBA. Very few make it, but everyone is willing to sell out everything important to achieve it. There has never been a person who ignored all the important things in life just to achieve a great career, who didn't regret it!

Patience with work helps to achieve the necessary balance between work and the other areas of life. Make sure you don't neglect the things most important to you.

WHATEVER YOUR WORK IS-- MAKE SURE YOU KEEP MONEY IN PERSPECTIVE!

Don't work for money. If you do, money will be all you get out of your work.

Money is the product of services rendered. What you earn should not be a reflection of your own worth. The trouble is, that is exactly how we measure our worth in our culture.

Further, we often think money is a result of production, rather than productivity. Production is concerned with results--productivity is concerned with how you got the results.

Whatever your work is--do your best. If you work hard at what you do, and enjoy it--the money will always come. Money is the product of services rendered.

WHATEVER YOUR WORK IS--BE A SERVANT!

Serve others. Put other people first. If you do this, you will always be able to keep your life in perspective. If you are ever going to feel like you are making a difference in your world, you have to feel like a servant. Try tracing all the areas of your work back to service. Think in terms of the people you are helping with your work. Every job makes someone's life better or easier. Make it your personal commitment to be working for them, not for you.

Make it your purpose in life to meet the needs of others. The freedom your spirit will experience as you work for the purpose of serving will enrich your life greater than any material possession ever could.

WHATEVER YOUR WORK IS--BE PATIENT WITH OTHERS IN THE WORK ENVIRONMENT!

Your personal success in the workplace is directly related to your ability to be patient with others. Impatience is often justified and fueled through various confrontations. Patience is most needed in the area of personal relationships.

There are so many variables when it comes to the success of people getting along with other people in the work place. Everyone carries around a certain amount of personal problems. When these problems are subconsciously or consciously focussed on someone else, the situation can become explosive.

Whether you are an employee or employer, your success with others will be directly proportionate to your patience with others.

CHAPTER 8: PATIENCE AT HOME

Ecclesiastes 9:7-10 "Go, eat your food with gladness, and drink your wine with a joyful heart, for it is now that God favors what you do. Always be clothed in white, and always anoint your head with oil. Enjoy life with your wife, whom you love, all the days of this meaningless life that God has given you under the sun-- all your meaningless days. For this is your lot in life and in your toilsome labor under the sun. Whatever your hand finds to do, do it with all your might, for in the grave, where you are going, there is neither working nor planning nor knowledge nor wisdom."

One of the greatest areas of difficulty today is in the ability of people to be patient with their own family.

Most of the time we find it possible to put on a mask and be kind and patient with others, but when it comes to those we love the most, we become very impatient.

Impatience at home is often the result of looking at other homes. The appeal for someone else's life has a greater appeal than your own. The more you look at others, the less satisfied you are with what you have. **Keep your eyes on your own front porch!** Discontent and dissatisfaction creep in slowly. As you keep your eyes on your own home, remember to make a conscious decision to be patient with your loved ones. The more patience you have, the greater potential for happiness you will have. Patience creates a nurturing atmosphere. Impatience creates a critical atmosphere. Creating a nurturing or critical atmosphere is up to every family member.

Patience at home requires some very simple and practical concepts.

Enjoyment. The first key to having patience at home is to enjoy your home. It does not matter if you eat hot dogs or steak, live in a shack or a mansion, or wear second hand clothes or designer label. Enjoy your life. Enjoy your family. Enjoy every single person God has placed in your life.

Rather than complain and be discontented, it is better to determine to be satisfied and enjoy every day-- enjoy every bite--enjoy every moment with your loved ones.

It is much better to enjoy your own life, and the way your life goes, rather than look at the enjoyment or apparent enjoyment of others. A big reason for discontentment is that people study and lust after what others have rather than spend the time enjoying and being thankful for what they do have.

It is important to view everything as gifts from God for us to enjoy. We must realize with thankfulness that we are where we are because of God's will. When He wants our lifestyle to change, He will see to it. This kind of acceptance of God's involvement in your life will help you to be less impatient with how things are going and more appreciative of all you have been through.

Righteousness. Righteousness means right living. The moral climate in our homes set the moral climate of the world. We choose who sets the moral climate of the home. If we decide to let the input of Hollywood change us, it will. If we decide not to let the input of Hollywood change us, it won't. Parents and children together make the decision to change the world together. The world is changed one home at a time.

Righteousness is possible in homes. Families who decide to live fair, honest, and respectably have already beaten one of the biggest enemies of the home: guilt. Guilt can ruin lives. A righteous life brings no guilt--only a clear conscious.

Guilt brings on all kinds of impatience because people are confused. Watching what your input is can change your whole attitude about life.

Security. Everyone needs to feel safe and secure. The cause of the deepest emotional/mental problems stems from insecurity. Family life needs to provide a safe and secure environment for the family members.

A feeling of safety comes from being able to feel loved and affirmed by others. This affirmation needs to be expressed openly between family members. No one should assume love just because a home is shared with other people. Love should be expressed verbally.

People are in need of being "built up" and appreciated. Life takes its toll on everyone. Often people feel torn down. Families need to build each other up.

Patience at home gives family members the time and space to heal, and the affirmation to feel an important part of something. Don't rush the process of healing or coming together as a family. Family life is built over the course of time.

In some families, no one wants to be the first to express love. The fear of rejection overcomes the need to be affirmed. Families can seek help from others for teaching and training in the area of nurturing one another.

Secure environments beget secure environments. Insecure environments beget insecure ones. Providing a place of security for loved ones will result in great benefits.

Moral Commitment. Be patient with your loved ones and satisfied with your spouse. God gave you your spouse. Be happy with your children. God gave them to you.

There is no way to soften the concept of commitment. Commitment requires both faith and fortitude. Commitment demands us to follow through with what we said we would do, regardless of the excuse.

Morality is the reflection of a culture--which, in turn, is the reflection of the home. We must set our minds on moral absolutes--there are some things right and some things wrong to do. If we don't set our minds on moral absolutes, then values are continually open for interpretation.

Society reflects our moral values--it doesn't set them. We set moral values. Moral values are set in the homes across America and around the world.

Every marriage starts with some kind of vow. If people would just honor their vow, most of the problems with moral values would be solved. People need to follow through with what they said they would do in the first place. Then we wouldn't need to think about how serious the issue of moral values is because morals would be managed by commitment to a vow.

Everyone has reasons why they can justify their impatience with their loved ones. Everyone can make a list illustrating where others fall short. Until we accept the responsibility of our own behavior and determine to be patient with our loved ones, we will never see any improvement. Patience at home demands our commitment to overcome our own urge to always be heard. When people have to be heard, rarely are they listening. No one is ever heard until they take the time to listen and hear others. Patience at home does not have to hold on to one point of view, but opens up to others. Yielding to the needs of others and putting them first revolutionizes the patience necessary for a family to succeed.

I WILL BE PATIENT AT HOME BY:

1. Making the decision to be more patient with those I love.

2. Stop looking for the weakness in others.

3. Start accepting responsibility for my own behavior and attitude.

4. Give people I love the space and love necessary to grow.

5. Affirm my loved ones verbally and physically.

6. Put others first.

7. Give in to other points of view- not just hold on to my own.

CHAPTER 9: MASTERING THE MOST IMPORTANT INGREDIENT OF PATIENCE: CONTENTMENT

1 Corinthians 7:17--"Never the less each one should retain the place in life that the Lord assigned to him and to which God has called him. This is the rule I lay down in all the churches."

Philippians 4:11-13--"I am not saying this because I am in need, for I have learned to be content whatever the circumstances. I know what it is to be in need, and I know what it is to have plenty. I have learned the secret of being content in any and every situation, whether well fed or hungry, whether living in plenty or in want. I can do everything through him who gives me strength."

Hebrews 13:5-6--"Keep your lives free from the love of money and be content with what you have, because God has said, "Never will I leave you; never will I forsake you." So we say with confidence, "The Lord is my helper; I will not be afraid. What can man do to me?"

1 Timothy 6:5-8--"..and constant friction between men of corrupt mind, who have been

robbed of the truth and who think that godliness is a means to financial gain. But godliness with contentment is great gain. For we brought nothing into the world, and we can take nothing out of it. But if we have food and clothing, we will be content with that."

Most people realize the need to be more content with their lives. About the time you decide it is better to be content, you hear a motivational speaker, window shop at the mall, or watch your neighbor drive home in a big new Sport Utility Vehicle.

Every piece of information we receive has to do with being more, accomplishing more, and having more. What we have is not big enough, good enough, or trendy enough. We are encouraged to get more stuff to keep up with others. No one wants to be left out.

Contentment is a tough road to navigate. There are so many potential reasons why we could be derailed from a contented life. The reason most people are not content is because they have never been taught how to be content.

Distractions in life often complicate the issue. A firm determination can be made to be more content, and then suddenly a job promotion comes, a new is car purchased, or a great sale on clothes changes the previous thought-through life change.

Learning to be content is a life-long journey. It is the first step in developing patience in your life. It is also a life filled with joy. Learning to be content requires the application of three very important changes.

FIRST:
TO MASTER CONTENTMENT IN YOUR LIFE YOU HAVE TO CHANGE THE WAY YOU THINK!

The normal process of thinking is to become bigger, better, and more ambitious. Motivational speakers tell us that the ambitious nature will take us anywhere we want to go. All that is needed to succeed is the desire and drive to succeed.

Along the road of this kind of ambitious thinking are all kinds of defeated, hurt, and broken people.

Success in life has to be based upon something more than numbers, quotas, standard of living, or money in the bank.

Many try to get on the right road to patience by being more contented with their situation in life, but seem to get no where. The unhappiest person in the world is the one who is dissatisfied with his or her "lot in life." These people suffer from the guilt of their own perceived errors. Maybe they felt they accepted the wrong job or got in a rush and married the wrong person. Others suffer from their own self-induced depression by blaming others for their life. It could be that a parent, spouse, or ex-spouse is the one blamed for the misery. All of these problems could be solved if we could just change our thinking about the situation. The truth is, nothing about the situation has to change--if your thinking changes--everything changes!

The way to change your thinking and become more content is by believing that **God is in complete control of any situation**. If God is in control, then you should relax, be content, and let Him take care of things. What you should do is stay put, wait on God, pray about the situation, turn it over to Him, and let God change direction or open other doors for you.

This change of thinking is not the lazy way out. Turning things over to God is not lazy. In fact, most people who do so realize that turning things over to God is hard work.

No matter what hurts you have had, the healing begins the moment you decide to change the way you think about the situation, and by turning it over to God.

It doesn't matter what decisions you have made up to this point in your life. Even if you have blown it time and again, there is always a point of correction up ahead. Turn it all over to God--wait for Him to direct you--and you will see that you will be back in God's perfect plan in short order.

The ultimate requirement for all this to happen is to submit to God. This means following and applying God's Word to your life. Every hurt, every mistake, every failure is correctable. Contentment begins the moment you turn every situation over to God.

SECOND:
TO MASTER CONTENTMENT IN YOUR LIFE YOU HAVE TO UNDERSTAND THAT "KNOCKING" IS A SPIRITUAL PRINCIPLE!

Jesus' great principle of Ask-Seek-Knock from the Sermon on the Mount is known worldwide. It has been applied to everything from fundraising for charities to selling used cars.

The simple idea of **"ask and you will receive, seek and you will find, knock and the door will be**

opened unto you," is never more real than when you apply it to a contented life.

The secret to being content and developing patience in your life is to understand that contentment means to knock on the doors of opportunity. When you contrast the idea of knocking on a door, then waiting for an answer with pushing, pulling, or prying a door open, you will see just how contentment works on a practical level of life.

When you knock on a door, you get one of two answers: either it opens or it doesn't. If it opens, that means go through. If it doesn't open, it means to stay on this side of the door. Can you be content and still continue to knock? Why not?! Knocking is a part of life. If you desire something, knock on the door of opportunity. Don't be hurt if it doesn't open. If you still desire it, continue to knock. Don't hurt your knuckles by pounding too hard!

Contentment comes into play when we realize we have worked hard and done everything possible to advance. If advancement comes, we see it as from God. If advancement does not come, we see that as from God as well. When the door doesn't open for you, it should be seen as from God and accepted as such.

Don't push or force doors open. Let the doors open up for you. Wait doors out. Timing is everything in life. God is in control of the timing. Knock loudly and

clearly on each door--don't ever use a hammer and a crow
bar.

THIRD:
TO MASTER CONTENTMENT IN YOUR LIFE YOU HAVE TO STAY FOCUSSED!

The idea of focussing means to center in on what
is important. Through the course of each day, we are
pulled back and forth one way and then another. It is easy
to lose our focus if we are not constantly aware of the
importance of retaining it.

Contentment can only be mastered if we lay out
and execute our priorities of personal conviction. The
only way contentment is possible is when contentment
and developing patience is a personal conviction in your
life.

All of us can go along for a while maintaining our
focus. Then something comes along with a higher
priority or sense of conviction. The new thing takes our
attention, and hence, our focus off the center of our
previous priority. Two reasons we often lose focus are
fear and pride. We fear many things, not the least of
which is people and what they think. Pride creates in us
an independent spirit rather than a dependency upon God.

Lust is a third reason we can lose focus. Lust of the flesh includes peer pressure, covetousness, jealousy, sexual temptation, material temptation, and fleshly desires.

If we let these desires grow, our focus blurs. Without clear focus, you cannot master contentment or develop patience in your life. Patience will always take you further than lust, pride, or fear. Contentment is not only possible, it is within each of us if we **change our thinking, knock, and focus!**

CHAPTER 10: DEVELOPING PATIENCE
THROUGH ADVERSITY

2 Corinthians 6:4-6--"Rather, as servants of God we commend ourselves in every way: in great endurance; in troubles, hardships and distresses; in beatings, imprisonments and riots; in hard work, sleepless nights and hunger; in purity, understanding, patience and kindness; in the Holy Spirit and in sincere love."

2 Timothy 2:3-7--"Endure hardship with us like a good soldier of Christ Jesus. No one serving as a soldier gets involved in civilian affairs--he wants to please his commanding officer. Similarly, if anyone competes as an athlete, he does not receive the victor's crown unless he competes according to the rules. The hardworking farmer should be the first to receive a share of the crops. Reflect on what I am saying, for the Lord will give you insight into all this."

Trying to develop patience is hard enough, but patience during the easy times is different from patience during the difficult times.

When times are difficult, survival is often the only thing you are thinking about. The truth is, it is during the difficult times that we are able to develop the greatest levels of patience. A large measure of the maturation process has to do with the development of patience.

There is a choice all of us have when facing adversity and hardship: We can either become hardened, bitter and resentful, or tender, seasoned, and moldable. Facing adversity brings out the better or worse in people. In adversity we either become more sensitive or increasingly bitter. Becoming bitter or more sensitive is a clear choice that is up to you!

There are some practical applications to help in making this choice. Adversity or hardship is never easy. We can prepare ahead of time to get ready for adverse circumstances. These concepts can help guide our thinking. These concepts are ordinary things that will simply help in the maturation process. They will help you grow during the tough times.

ACT AND SPEAK HONORABLY

Don't do or say anything that you will later regret or feel embarrassed about. Be honest. Speak the truth.

You have to make the conscious decision ahead of time to be honest and speak honestly. If the decision is not made ahead of time, you will feel threatened by the moment and lie. When adversity comes, it is often easier to give in to your own sense of fear, than to be honest. If you give in, you will stagnate in your life and not grow from adversity.

Develop a sense of respect. Be respectful to others. Banish sarcasm from your life and speak affirming words to others. If you determine this ahead of time, you will not be pulled down at the time of your own adversity and say dishonorable things.

Consistently execute kindness in everything you do. Let kindness be your most consistent attribute. It is the outward expression of Christian love. Kindness will also help you develop a greater depth of patience in your life. If you are consistent in being kind in all circumstances, you will have no trouble staying kind during adverse times in your life.

ENDURE LIKE A SOLDIER IN BATTLE

Most of the time hardship requires a gruesome amount of endurance. The most enduring attitude in the world is that of a soldier. The soldier has a purpose, a cause, and a focus. This same posture should be true of any person wanting to develop patience through adversity in his/her life.

The Vietnam War was fought in the jungles of Asia. Many of the men have some amazing stories of endurance that have never been told. One such story was that of a foot soldier who spent days in a rice paddy field after being shot down. He had to spend a month in a pool of salt and mineral water to kill the ringworm that had infested every inch of his body. The injuries he suffered caused what the doctors thought to be permanent damage. They told him he would never walk again. Through his personal endurance and struggles, this man was a varsity high school basketball coach within five years. Not only did he regain his ability to walk--he was jogging ten miles a day!

Personal endurance is often the only thing that will see you through. Adversity and hardship must be viewed as battles we face as soldiers in the course of life. We must endure hardship to develop a depth of patience. The patience we develop will help us face greater levels of adversity down the road.

SEEK TO PLEASE GOD

Anyone who faces adversity must know ahead of time who it is they are going to please. Determining whom you are going to please ahead of time will prevent confusion when facing adversity.

It takes a sincere heart and a submitted spirit to please God, but that is all it takes. The best way to please God is to practice the presence of God in your personal life. The idea that He is right here, right now--and all the time--allows us to think of God in personal and present terms.

PERSONAL REFLECTION

The final concept to develop patience through adversity is to reflect on your inner life. Internalize the things that happen to you. Learn from your mistakes. While undergoing something difficult, always take the time to reflect and internalize it. Reflect honestly. Honesty will help you develop maturity. It will also help you develop a depth of character.

CHAPTER 11: THE ETERNAL REWARD OF A PATIENT LIFE

Romans 2:7--"To those who by persistence in doing good seek glory, honor and immortality, he will give eternal life."

Luke 21:19--"By standing firm you will gain life."

Romans 8:25--"But if we hope for what we do not yet have, we wait for it patiently."

The idea of eternity is a big subject. It refers to the eons of time in the great beyond. We all have an interest in eternity since we have a hope of a life after this one.

It all comes down to this: **The whole purpose of developing patience is eternal!** The goal in this life is to become all we can be with eternity in mind. Our life's goals need to go farther, grow deeper, and be greater than just the benefits for the here and now.

The great heroes of faith believed strongly in investing this earthly life for the sake of eternal life. No sacrifice was too great to them to keep eternity first. It is not fatalistic at all to dedicate one's life here for the good of the next one. The philosopher Blaise Pascal said, "It is not foolish for a man to believe in that which he has the most to gain compared to the least to lose."

The hope of every Christian is the destiny of heaven in the great beyond. The conscientious person lives life to the betterment of the soul with hopes of it making a difference in the life beyond.

There are three ideas that capture this hope of eternal life and allow the development of patience to be something you take with you: persistence, firmness, and waiting.

PERSISTENCE. The greatest part of a life of faith is actually the testing of it. During a test, you are able to see what you are really made of. Persistence is the key to any kind of success. No one is ever perfect at anything all of the time, but persistence eventually brings success. It is never how good you are, but how persistent you are.

The practice of faith is not a public, open endeavor. Practicing faith is personal and private. Our faith is the most personal thing we have in our lives. Only you know if you have been persistent in the practicing of your faith.

It is obvious if someone has been persistent in how he or she holds up under a trial or test. The tests and trials in life come in many different forms. The tests vary in intensity and effect.

Persistence is often displayed through a person's lifestyle. If one follows the world's system of values, one's morals will be in a constant degenerative pattern. If one applies persistence to a positive lifestyle, one will be able to see a great depth of patience in his or her life.

FIRMNESS. Firmness applies to the area of personal conviction. Each of us must draw lines in many areas of life. These drawn lines are created from those deep convictions we feel. How firm we stand is really how deep our convictions run.

Firmness is deeply personal. We cannot dictate to each other what to be firm about or how to be firm in each area. Allow conviction to rise up and become the firmness needed in the boundaries of life.

In this day and age, the level of our firmness will determine the amount of conviction we will pass on to the future generations. However, the populace often rebels against people with conviction. Being firm often means being unpopular or politically incorrect. Remember: firmness/conviction is an eternal concept, not a temporal one. People who live only in the temporal world will never understand those living for eternity.

WAITING. Waiting upon God could be compared to weight lifting and the football player--it is training for fitness.

Waiting upon God provides the soul with strength and depth. Part of this strength comes from the day to day dynamics of having to wait upon God for meeting needs.

Waiting is often grueling. Waiting is uncomfortable to say the least. When we pray, the answer is always yes, no or **"wait"!** Our strength is determined by how patiently we wait upon God.

Waiting is easier if we view life as a journey. Along the road are many choices. There are many kinds of roads. Some roads are long and hard, some are short and wide. Some roads are just short cuts. We don't have to succumb to the pitfalls of life. Our journey can be one of peace, joy and patience--but only if we wait upon God.

We are all pilgrims on this journey. Some are more talented--others more gifted--some smarter--some prettier--some better connected. As pilgrims, we all have something in common--we all need more patience than we possess. Each person needs to support and encourage the other. There is plenty of patience to go around--let's start developing some!

DEVELOPING PATIENCE IS BEST SEEN AS AN ETERNAL WORK WE DO WHILE ON THE JOURNEY OF LIFE!

" For everything that was written in the past was written to teach us, so that through endurance and the encouragement of the Scriptures we might have hope." Romans 15:4

"But the seed on good soil stands for those with a noble and good heart, who hear the word, retain it, and by persevering produce a crop." Luke 8:15

"The things that mark an apostle--signs, wonders and miracles--were done among you with great perseverance." 2 Corinthians 12:12

99